The Pedagogy

of Praise

The Pedagogy of Praise

How Congregational Worship
Shapes Christian Character

Jeffrey P. Greenman

Regent College Publishing

Published 2016 by Regent College Publishing
5800 University Boulevard,
Vancouver, BC V6T 2E4 Canada

Regent College Publishing is an imprint of the Regent
Bookstore <www.regentbookstore.com>. Views expressed in
works published by Regent College Publishing are those of the
author and do not necessarily represent the official position of
Regent College <www.regent-college.edu>.

ISBN 978-1-57383-532-9

Cataloguing in Publication information is available from
Library and Archives Canada.

All Scripture citations are from NIV unless otherwise cited.
Scripture citations labeled ESV are taken from the English
Standard Version.

Book layout and cover design by
The Dunbar Group, LLC / www.DunbarPublishing.com

For Tony Payne
Churchman, musician, collaborator, friend

Contents

Preface

This book is meant to help Christians make connections between Sunday worship and the rest of life. Its ultimate aim is that more Christians around the world would be better equipped to live out a deeper, more integrated faith.

It has been designed for reading in a single sitting. The book is deliberately short, in order that it might be read by a wide audience of Christians who care about worship, discipleship, spiritual growth, and Christian character. There is a series of short chapters, most of which are focused on suggesting some implications of one element in the full scope of components incorporated in the Sunday worship services of Christendom. In some cases, my brief discussion of an enormously complex topic (for instance, the Lord's Supper) begs for more elaboration, and has been limited to consideration of the topic only from the perspective of questions about spiritual-moral formation.

Preface

I invite you to pour yourself a nice cup of coffee, find a comfortable chair, and follow along on a journey.

It is not a book aimed primarily at ministry specialists or theological experts, but has been written for "regular Christians" looking for challenge and encouragement. The book should be suitable for discussion in adult education courses, discipleship programs, and small groups. I hope it proves useful for students in bible schools, Christian universities, or theological colleges. It should also benefit worship leaders, music directors, and pastors who are looking for material that could enrich their understanding of congregational worship.

It is my pleasure to dedicate the book to my longtime friend and former colleague at Wheaton College, Dr. Tony L. Payne. It has been my joy and privilege to collaborate in various ways with Tony, whose rare gifts as a teacher, choir master, composer, arranger, and impresario are exercised with remarkable humility, warmth, and intelligence.

Introduction

Growing up as a churchgoing and Sunday school–attending child, I became familiar with congregational worship at an early age. In my family's mainline Protestant tradition, participation in weekly liturgical worship was a given. In some ways, it was taken for granted. Sunday morning worship in church was there, and it was something we did because it was important. Certainly it was taken seriously. But as far as I can recall, it was not something we talked much about. In particular, I do not think that anyone ever explained to me why the service was the way it was. What was really going on with the various hymns, readings, sermons, and prayers? And what did this experience of Sunday worship have to do with the rest of the week?

I am deeply grateful for my "churched" background. It prepared me in more ways than I can possibly realize to take a personal step of faith at age twenty-two. We absorb more than we know, and we "know" a great deal by experience. Surely the cumulatively beneficial effect of ongoing exposure to congregational worship played an important role in preparing my heart and mind for a fresh experience of the gospel. By the grace of God, my conversion to Christ brought into vivid colour what had been like a black-and-white picture. The Christian picture was familiar, to be sure, yet faith in Christ meant that the reality of what was depicted simply sprang to life as never before. Many people can attest to this type of spiritual encounter.

For me, commitment to Christ meant taking my long-standing academic and personal interests in ethics, character, and public life and reorienting them toward Christ. As historian Andrew Walls has written, conversion "is about turning what is already there; it is more about direction than content."[1] For me, it meant asking new questions. From my studies of philosophy, I had adopted the ancient Greek way of thinking about ethics—namely, as best organized around the question, "What is the best sort of life for human beings to live?" Their typical answer was that there is a way of human flourishing, expressed through core virtues, that is consistent with human nature, in fulfillment of the most important purposes of life. There is a great deal of value in that framework for thinking about the moral life. Plenty of other ethical

---

1. Andrew F. Walls, "The Ephesian Moment," in *The Cross-Cultural Process in Christian History* (Maryknoll, NY: Orbis Books, 2002), 79.

approaches fail to capture nearly as much truth about the moral life.

However, in Christian terms that approach does not go far enough. It is not only incomplete, but also its foundation is inadequate because it arises from a narrative that is sub-Christian. The pagan pursuit of virtue is not to be scorned, but pagan virtue is simply not the same thing as biblical faithfulness. The gospel calls women and men to faith in Jesus Christ, to live in distinctive ways as his disciples through the work of the Holy Spirit. Christians are called to become "like Christ," which means sharing in the character of God himself, imitating Jesus, whose life is the supreme expression of humble, self-giving love. What does genuine human flourishing look like from the standpoint of the gospel? What is the best sort of life, if we seek to be people whose lives are pleasing to God? What kinds of virtues are central to the Christian story of faith? What does it mean to follow after Christ into the world? These are critically important questions, ones that arise naturally from orthodox theological convictions.

As a scholar and teacher in theology and ethics, my main concern has been exploring the questions, What difference does Christian faith make for life in the world? For the way Christians live as parents, children, and citizens? For our lives at work and at play? For our use of money, our hobbies, or what we eat? The key assumption here is that Christianity is not a set of theoretical insights or an abstract philosophy, but an embodied, communal way of life with relevance to every aspect of daily existence and human culture. And if Christianity is true, so what? What difference would it make to the way we live? And how might we become the kinds of people who live out their faith in all spheres of life with integrity and authenticity?

This book brings together reflection on congregational worship with questions of moral formation. What role does participation in Sunday worship play in making us more like Christ? What importance does worship have for the formation of Christian character, the very heart of our spiritual-moral lives?[2]

There are many contexts through which God commonly works to shape Christian character. Certainly the home is a central place where the practices and example of religious family life can either enhance or impede the growth of faith. Likewise, friendship plays a major role in coming to understand God, to grasp God's ways, and to live out one's faith. Additionally, the personal disciplines of Bible reading and prayer can be deeply formative. Christian education programs or church-based small groups also have been important for many people as they grow toward maturity as Christians. The rationale for this

---

2. Our attention will focus on the regular experience of weekly worship, excluding other important non-weekly practices of worship such as baptism, foot washing, or marriage.

book is that one context that is less commonly discussed is the context of communal worship. The present study aims to address this particular gap by exploring how congregational worship can shape Christian character. In doing so, I do not mean to suggest that these other contexts are unimportant, nor to imply that congregational worship is, by itself, more important than anything else for everyone. A full treatment of the topic of moral-spiritual formation would give attention to each of these contexts. Rather, my point is that the dynamics of congregational worship are powerfully formative and have not received as much attention as they deserve.

Spiritual Formation and Christian Character

Our exploration of the role congregational worship plays in character formation can be assisted by spelling out biblically grounded and theologically robust understandings of the interrelated subjects of spiritual formation, worship, and Christian character.

The place to start is with spiritual formation. To my mind, this is virtually interchangeable with moral formation. Thus, sometimes I will use a hyphenated construction to refer to one unified reality: spiritual-moral formation. The reason is that the Bible does not make a distinction between the spiritual and moral realms, or between spiritual and moral questions. There is not a "spiritual" realm that is somehow disembodied or disconnected from the totality of someone's life experience. There is not a "moral" realm that somehow singles out an aspect of human life that is independent of, or separable from, the spiritual realities of the universe and the spiritual nature of human beings as made in God's image. In Scripture, all our conduct in words and deeds are spiritual-and-moral matters in the lives of persons. Our moral choices reflect our spiritual orientation, either demonstrating our allegiance to the true and living God or our allegiance to some other god. We give concrete expression to the content of our hearts and souls through our speech and action. It is best to think persistently in terms of human beings as whole persons: embodied and relational spiritual-moral-thinking-feeling beings who live in God's world as his creatures, and who are called by faith to know, trust, follow, and obey the Triune God who is their Creator and Redeemer.

How should we understand Christian spiritual formation for creatures such as ourselves? In another context I offered the following definition:

> Spiritual formation is our continuing response to the reality of God's grace shaping us into the likeness of Jesus Christ, through the work of the Holy Spirit, in the community of faith, for the sake of the world.[1]

1. Jeffrey P. Greenman, "Spiritual Formation in Theological Perspective: Classic Issues, Contemporary Challenges," in *Life in the Spirit: Spiritual Formation in Theological Perspective*, eds. Jeffrey P. Greenman and George Kalantzis (Downers Grove, IL: IVP Academic, 2010), 24.

For our purposes, a brief explanation of this definition will be sufficient. Spiritual formation is a matter of *continuing response* because we are speaking of a lifelong journey of faith that calls Christians to pay ongoing attention to God by exercising their faith and trust. It is vital to see spiritual formation as a response to the reality of God's grace rather than as a self-generated quest for spiritual improvement that comes from merely human willpower or effort. The ultimate goal of spiritual formation is *being shaped into the likeness of Jesus Christ*. It is not a process of "becoming a better you" or "fulfilling your innate potential" but is rather growth into conformity to the pattern shown us by Jesus, whose earthly life revealed the way of true human flourishing. This kind of deep-seated transformation is a result of the work of the Holy Spirit in us. Christian growth involves our cooperation with God's Spirit, but it is not merely a human project of willpower. The Spirit ministers God's powerful presence, doing in us what is needed most and what only God himself can do. Spiritual formation is best undertaken not in isolation as atomized individuals, but *in the community of faith*. Part of that means participating in congregational worship, which is the focus in our study. This type of formation, which at the same time glorifies God and transforms individuals to become more like Christ, is *for the sake of the world*, in the sense that it sends Christians into active service in the world as God's representatives and witnesses.

This definition points us toward a theological framework for thinking about Christian character. To develop Christian character is to become like Christ, which is what we have called a process of spiritual-moral formation. Character is a matter of the whole person. It refers to our way of being in the world, encompassing our ways of thinking (using our minds and imaginations), our ways of feeling, and our ways of reacting to what happens to us. Character speaks to our desires, aspirations, and affections. It includes our ways of acting, choosing, behaving, treating others, and treating ourselves. It reflects our motivations and intentions. Therefore, we can say that character is who we are, deep down, as persons, and how that is expressed. The best shorthand summary might be, "Character is who you are when no one is watching." It expresses our true self. Character is a trait of human lives that is stable, enduring, and ongoing. Our character develops gradually over time. Character can change and grow, but for most adults, it is relatively persistent in a changing world and in diverse contexts.

If so, what is *Christian* character? It is becoming like Christ in all these ways: being people whose minds, hearts, wills, affections, motivations, intentions, and actions are shaped by Christ and reflect who Christ is and what he has done. Christian character is capable of growth and development, by God's grace, through the work of the Holy Spirit, with whom Christians are invited to cooperate in a life of faith and trust. Christian character means that our human lives take on the qualities and attributes of God's own character, as shown in Jesus. We become more like God himself, reflecting his character in the world, which was the original purpose of our creation in the divine image.

Where does worship fit into this picture? While my focus is on congregational worship, we need to distinguish it from what I will call "worship in the fullest sense." In biblical terms, the whole of our lives is meant to be worship, in the broad sense of being offered to God. The great text along these lines is Romans 12:1, which after the magnificent exposition of God's saving purposes in chapters 9–11, states: "Therefore, I urge you, brothers and sisters, in view of God's mercy, to offer your bodies as a living sacrifice, holy and pleasing to God—this is your true and proper worship." In the splendid rendering of Eugene Peterson in *The Message*, it reads: "So here's what I want you to do, God helping you: Take your everyday, ordinary life—your sleeping, eating, going-to-work, and walking-around life—and place it before God as an offering." Using these categories, we can say that my interest is what *congregational* worship has to do with worship in the *fullest* sense. How does what we do during Sunday gathering equip us for life on Monday through Saturday? How does the gathered life of the church prepare God's people for their scattered life? Worship in the profound, fullest, all-of-life sense is a matter of living out, day by day, with intentionality and purpose, an integrated, undivided, joined-up life of faithfulness. It is taking our whole being, and all our beings, and offering ourselves to God, to his service, for the sake of his praise, honour, and glory. Doing that involves being a person of Christian character, a person in Christ marked by a deeply Christian identity.

My argument is that this profile of godly character is deeply shaped in and through congregational worship. Formation through communal worship is a necessary condition for spiritual maturity; we cannot reasonably expect to experience a deeply Christian identity without it.

This brings us to what we should consider the very heart of congregational worship. Given that there are many ways of understanding what is "worship" on Sunday mornings, we need to pause briefly to clarify what constitutes Christian worship. My favourite definition is provided by Horton Davies, a premiere historian of the church's long tradition of worship. He writes:

> Worship is the glad homage of mind, heart, imagination and conscience offered by the Body of Christ to its Lord as a response to revelation. The mind is open to the truth of God in Scripture and sermon. The imagination is enthralled by the majesty of God, Creator and Redeemer, in symbolism, architecture, music and the sacraments. The heart is overjoyed by the forgiving love of God and by the fellowship of

the redeemed in heaven and on earth. The conscience
is opened and purified by the commands of God and
the example and teachings of our Lord. The entire
personality in community is educated in the prayers
of adoration, confession, petition, intercession and
consecration, so that we are elevated, abased, judged
and driven forth in sacrificial service to the world.[2]

This is an excellent definition. Allow me to offer a few
observations about the significance of Davies's rich and
compelling account. Worship is homage—paying due
tribute, reverence, and respect to One who is worthy. It is a
response to revelation, in recognition of God's own initia-
tive in grace and mercy toward his world. We worship on
the basis of what is known by divine revelation, not on the
basis of human speculation. Worship is the engagement
of the whole person ("mind, heart, imagination and conscience"), a matter of "the entire personality in community." Davies holds together what we so often tear apart,
namely, the individual and the communal dimensions of
worship. Quite rightly Davies also sees that worship is a
matter of being "educated" as Christians. This means that
something formative is involved, a process of growth and
learning and transformation. This point squares with the
New Testament's emphasis that communal worship is to

2. Quoted in Paul Ramsey, "Liturgy and Ethics," *Journal of Religious
Ethics* 7, no. 2 (1979), 139–171, at 146.

be "edifying" to the people assembled. (At the very least, this runs counter to our contemporary temptation to see worship as a form of entertainment or spectacle.) This educative emphasis is also reflected in my title, *The Pedagogy of Praise*, referring to the ways that our shared practices of praise in worship teach us as Christians. It refers to the whole scope of spiritual engagement ("adoration, confession, petition, intercession, and consecration"). Worship keeps an active, missional horizon in view, "sacrificial service to the world."

At this point we need to insist upon an important point of theological precision. Congregational worship is not *about* us, nor *for* us. It is *about* God and *for* God—for the sake of his honour, glory, and praise. Our formation or education or edification is a by-product of Godward worship. We do not aim directly at our transformation, but we do what we do knowing that it should edify us and build up our faith. We aim to offer worthy praise to the Triune God, knowing that our good and benefit and blessing is found in his praise. In the words of philosopher James K. A. Smith: "The point of worship is not our formation; rather, formation is the overflow of our encounter with the Redeemer in praise and prayer, adoration and communion."[3] This mindset prevents worship from devolving

3. James K. A. Smith, *Desiring the Kingdom: Worship, Worldview, and Cultural Formation* (Grand Rapids: Baker, 2009), 150.

into something merely functional or utilitarian, an orchestrated means to the end of spiritual growth.

Similarly, there is a world of difference between walking to the beach to see a magnificently beautiful vista at sunset and walking to the beach for the sake of exercise. In the first case, we know we will get exercise and it will be good for us. But that is not why we walked there. We went for the view, perhaps even to admire the beauty of God's creation and to give praise to the Creator for his handiwork. The walk is secondary and might not even be much on our minds. In the second case, the sunset is incidental. The vista is not our focus. It is an almost arbitrary destination. The walk is what is on our minds. The exercise is what we really want. And so the beach experience is evaluated on the basis of whether we get the exercise we want, regardless of the view. The same principle applies to congregational worship. We participate in Sunday worship knowing that it is something good for us, just as walking to the beach promotes health. But that is not the main reason we go. We are drawn with the gathered community of faith for the vista—for the sake of God, for his honour, glory, and praise. Therefore the key question at the end of the service is not, "Did we have a good time?" but rather, "Was God honoured and glorified by our praises today?" If there is any valid question about ourselves to be asked, it might be, "Did we offer ourselves to the Lord today?" This changes the equation from the self-focused question of what we "got out of it" to the Godward-focused question of what we gave to the Lord.

One way to express clearly the dynamics and purpose of congregational worship is to use some logical categories made famous by the ancient Greek philosopher Aristotle. He distinguished four different kinds of causes. He was really talking about four different kinds of explanations for something, or four different kinds of "Why?" questions that we might ask about an object. One of the most famous illustrations is a bronze statue.

The final cause is the purpose, ultimate end, or goal for the sake of which something is done. The bronze statue was meant to honour a great hero. Why is the statue the way it is? Because it was built to pay tribute to or glorify a certain person, depicting them in a strong, positive manner.

The material cause is "that out of which" the statue is made, which is the bronze material itself. Why is the statue the way it is? Because it is made of bronze, not some other material.

The formal cause is the "form" or the "account of what-it-is-to-be," which in this case is the shape of the statue expressed in a blueprint or set of drawings or written instructions about how it is to be made. Why is the statue the way it is? Because it was made according to a certain design plan.

The efficient cause is the "primary source of change or rest," involving the making of the statue. In this case, an artisan who knows how to make bronze statues is the person who built it. Why is it the way it is? Because a certain craftsman made it that way.

The same logical analysis can be applied to Christian worship in order to help us understand the operative dynamics.

The final cause in worship is to offer praise, honour, and glory to the Triune God. That is the ultimate purpose for congregations as they gather Sunday by Sunday.

The material cause involves what we might call the "raw materials" of worship, namely, hymns, songs, Scripture readings, prayers, a sermon, and so on. Any given worship service is composed of these common elements in varying degrees.

The formal cause in worship is the sequence of elements, the theological design or order of service in place for the gathering.

The efficient cause should rightly be attributed to the work of the Holy Spirit, whose power and life-giving dynamism animates the congregants to offer worship in spirit and in truth (John 4:23–24). Of course there are human agents involved. People lead songs, play instruments, read Scripture, and preach sermons. But unless God's Spirit is the real agent at work in and through these human agents, we would not be able to worship rightly, and we would not be transformed by God's grace.

Here is a simple chart to display the comparison:

Type	Meaning	Bronze statue	Worship
Final cause	Purpose, end, goal	Honour a national hero	Glorify and honour God
Material cause	Materials used	Bronze of the statue	Song, prayer, sermon, etc.
Formal cause	Design, planned form	Shape given to it	Order of service
Efficient cause	Source of the change	Sculptor	Holy Spirit

This analysis sets the stage for us to consider the particular theological shape of Sunday worship. If glorifying God through song, prayer, sermon (and more) through the work of the Holy Spirit is the overall framework for congregational worship, what role does the specific content of the order of service play in shaping Christian lives?

2

The Theological Shape of Formative Worship

It should be clear that I am assuming that congregational worship consists of a variety of elements or components, including hymns, songs, prayers, Scripture readings, a sermon, and the Lord's Supper. "Worship" therefore does not refer primarily or exclusively to what the music team does, despite recent trends in evangelical Protestant circles. "Worship" is not reducible to singing, but refers to the entirety of what an "order of service" offers to God in response to his grace.

In addition, throughout this book I am not assuming that a particular pattern of worship is necessarily best, nor that a "liturgical" model is superior. Congregational worship always follows some order or pattern, whether or not it is written down. Some traditions such as Roman Catholics, Anglicans, or Presbyterians use a set form of words for their prayers and praises. Others such as Plymouth Brethren, Pentecostal, or Quaker do not. For my purposes, the key question is about the theological direction and flow of the order of service being used. Is that order truly reflective of the gospel? Does it reflect the revealed truth about the nature and character of God?

Worship that honours God and edifies his people should have a distinct theological shape. Every service of worship has a beginning, middle, and end. There is always an order, a logic, and a flow that gives a shape to the experience. There is always someone (a pastor, a worship leader, a liturgical author) who composes an order with a particular theological direction in mind. The rationale reflected in an order makes all the difference. My contention is simply that weekly congregational worship should be intentionally, deliberately, clearly, and transparently God-centred. It should celebrate who God is, what he has done, and what he has promised to do in the future. At the heart of this experience is re-presenting and re-experiencing the gospel each week. This does not mean issuing an evangelical "altar call" with each sermon. Rather it means rehearsing the good news of what God has accomplished in the incarnation, death, resurrection, and ascension of Jesus Christ.

I argue that there should be a fourfold design to congregational worship, built around the alternating dynamics of revelation and response. This insight is at the core of historic, orthodox Christian worship. There is a simple yet powerful "theological logic" that provides structured balance that both honours God and edifies his people. The basic pattern begins with a recognition of God's nature and character, who God is and what he has done, chiefly expressed in objective affirmations that are declarations of Trinitarian praise. Then follows a cycle of recognition of sin, reminders of God's grace, and expressions of faith and trust. Each of these elements can feature readings, prayers, or songs—there is no set formula that is necessarily best. But the God-sin-grace-faith flow is at the heart of God-centred, orthodox worship.

A prime example is found in Thomas Cranmer's shaping of the sixteenth-century Anglican Book of Common Prayer, though the same pattern can be found in other traditions. Theologian J. I. Packer has identified a distinct theological cycle at the heart of historic Anglican worship, which gives it a "built-in evangelical design" or clear gospel shape. He writes that this pattern means that

> to join in a service of worship is to be taken on a journey through a prescribed series of thoughts and actions. How did Cranmer secure evangelical worship? By routing his regular services via a sequence of three themes: first, the detecting and confessing of sin; second, the announcing of grace, in God's promise to pardon and restore the penitent through Christ; third, the exercising of faith, first in believing

> God's promise and trusting him for pardon, and then in acts of praise, testimony, intercession, and obeying instruction, all based on the prior restoring of fellowship with God through forgiveness.[1]

The result is a fresh experience of the gospel, which honours God's grace and forms his people to become gospel-shaped in their own character as a response of faith.

The logic of this cycle can be depicted as follows:

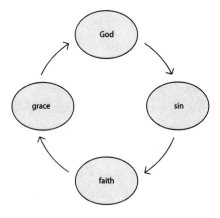

Such a simple yet powerful theological pattern in Sunday worship sets an important example for the congregation as a whole and for each participant. The language of corporate of worship naturally becomes the language of our faith experience, carried over into all realms of life.

1. J. I. Packer, "The Gospel in the Prayer Book," Reformed Anglican Fellowship, http://www.reformedanglican.us/blog/2014/1/9/the-gospel-in-the-prayer-book. Accessed August 23, 2016.

For instance, if communal worship is strongly biblical in its focus, whereby in-depth seriousness about Scripture is exemplified, then it is likely that people will come to highly value the Bible and its teaching. That will inform their other values and their personal priorities to be people who hear and receive God's Word in Scripture. On the other hand, if a congregation's public prayers are exclusively for physical needs or natural calamities, but not for evangelism or spiritual growth, then that practice sends a strong message about what is most important in prayer. A common adage is, "Children learn what they live." The same principle applies to congregations. Congregants learn what is lived out in their midst, Sunday by Sunday. What exemplary women and men of faith demonstrate before us rubs off on us and sticks in our hearts and minds. A great deal of communication is implicit. All this means that worship leaders, whether they are pastors or lay people, should give careful attention to what is being modeled for the congregation, since modeling has such power to shape people's outlooks, aspirations, and attitudes.

A clear implication of this brief theological account is that not all worship is created equal. Not all worship has equal potential to honour God or to be formative of truly Christian character. Truth be told, some expressions of worship can be deformative or even corrupting. Misshapen worship can generate unfortunate outcomes, including misshapen Christian character. A few examples illustrate the point that worship can go wrong in a variety of ways.

If the songs, preaching, and prayers of congregational worship tend to be me-centred rather than God-centred, the unfortunate result is formation toward becoming turned in on ourselves, focused on ourselves, or even self-absorbed amid the cultural pressures toward self-focus in Western society. This has serious implications for Christian morality: we find ways to justify our self-preoccupation or even selfishness. In some evangelical Protestant circles, there is a danger of overemphasizing our subjective response of faith at the expense of the object of our faith. Again, there is detrimental effect on morality: we find ways to rationalize our feelings and to defend our actions as "what felt right to us." In God-centred worship, we do not celebrate our feelings; we celebrate who God is and what he has done.

If these central elements of communal worship are insufficiently Trinitarian—for instance, through the conspicuous absence of the Holy Spirit from songs, preaching, and prayers—then the gospel is distorted and the Triune God is not adequately praised. Additionally, there are plenty of possible distortions around the identity and work of Jesus Christ. The incarnate God-man Jesus can be portrayed either as insufficiently divine or insufficiently human, with dire consequences in either case for the content of worship, and equally dire consequences for Christian living.[2]

If a particular congregation's pattern of worship tends toward being one-sidedly works-oriented, the wonder of divine grace is short-changed, with the result that Christian character is misshaped toward a performance-based, "earn God's rewards by doing good deeds" type of activism. The emphasis can turn quickly toward becoming a better person through our own moral effort (usually with a little bit of God's help) rather than recognizing ourselves as sinners in need of forgiveness and the healing power of the Spirit, people whose good works are the fruit of lives shaped deeply by faith in Christ.

2. For more insights along these lines, see C. FitzSimons Allison, *The Cruelty of Heresy: An Affirmation of Christian Orthodoxy* (Harrisburg, PA: Moorehouse, 1994).

3

Ordered Worship, Ordered Lives

The preceding discussion of formation, character, and the theology of worship sets the stage for us to consider how each element in a standard order of service might contribute to the spiritual-moral formation of congregants.

My discussion will address each component, although few services will include each element in each service. Some traditions emphasize some components far more than others. The exact order or sequence of elements is not my concern here (although the book unfolds along the lines of a sequence that I find most helpful and theologically satisfactory). Due to constraints of space, I will not be able to give a full treatment to each component. My focus will be on suggesting some of the most important moral implications of a set of specific worship practices. In doing so, we should bear in mind that the whole is far more than the sum of the parts. For the sake of analysis, we will treat these elements as separate features, isolating their potential contributions to moral formation. The risk is distorting the whole by isolating the parts. The lived experience of communal worship expresses these features in flowing connection with each other. We do not stop at each step in a given service to explain the element, to analyze what we are doing and what it means. It is helpful to remember that each element plays its own role in contributing to a cohesive whole, and to bear in mind that the cumulative effect of a series of components bears enormous potential for shaping the hearts and minds of worshippers as they give praise and honour to the Triune God. Ultimately, the experience of worship is central in shaping a clear and deep sense of Christian identity among God's people.

4

Gathering

What does your congregation do to begin a service of worship? What is said and done purposefully to gather people? How are the assembled people identified? What terms are used to define what we are doing when we gather? Is the name of God invoked? If so, how?

These questions matter because the initial gathering of people has everything to do with fundamental issues of personal and communal identity. People live and act as spiritual-moral beings out of their sense of identity, which inevitably involves their sense of how they belong to a group or organization. Therefore some clear intentionality about how we begin communal worship services is vitally important.

Some ways of gathering and greeting would encourage worrisome spiritual-moral malformation, such as: "Hi everyone. Are you ready for a good time?" That kind of opening can only encourage a spectator's consumerist identity. The problem is not relative informality but instead the misdirection of everyone's attention onto themselves rather than toward God. Instead, a morally formative practice would be to identify in whose name we gather—the Triune God's name. For example, in simple and familiar terms: "The grace of our Lord Jesus Christ, the love of God and the fellowship of the Holy Spirit be with you."

It would be positively formative to articulate why we are gathering at all. Why are we here? Not for a social event or "good time" together but for a specific set of spiritually grounded reasons. Accordingly, the worship leader might say, "We gather in the name of God as God's own people to offer him praise, to hear his Word, to be fed at his table, to pray for the needs of the world, and to be strengthened for his service." This kind of gathering reinforces the sense of belonging as a community to a distinct people who are present in response to God's invitation. We are people whose purpose in being together is God-centred. We are not a social club of people who choose one another's company for the sake of mutual enjoyment. We are not strangers to one another randomly collected as at a bus stop, but the body of Christ, those who belong to each other in a more profound way than any social club can offer. Our social, economic, racial, and ethnic identities are secondary to our primary identity as God's people. Being rich or poor, healthy or sick, young or old, white or black, and so on, do not form the basis for our gathering, nor the core of our personal identity.

A focused practice of gathering and greeting in these God-centred and community-reinforcing ways has formative significance in several related ways. It serves to counteract the increasing narcissism of Western culture, which glamourizes our fixation with ourselves and our preoccupation with our own feelings and experiences as if they were the most important things ever. People are reminded that a God-centred focus of Sunday worship is indicative of the direction and purpose of life as a whole. At the same time, congregants are reminded that our identity is found in belonging to God and to his people. This practice defies the individualism that so easily shapes our sense of identity and that creates the conditions for lost, lonely individuals who are cut off from friendship and communal support.

5

Praise and Thanks

Worship starts with God, is focused on God, and is a response to the revelation of who God is. The communal discipline of giving praise and thanks to the true and living Triune God is central to the identity of Christian disciples. Christians are people who have received the divine gift of a new centre of life and a new focus of their love in Jesus Christ. Any community gathered in his name is called to recognize who God is, what he has done, and what he has promised to accomplish according to his perfect purposes. This is why declarative praise is the centre point of congregational worship. We profess the truth about the Creator and Redeemer God, that "the Lord is gracious and merciful, slow to anger and abounding in steadfast love" (Ps. 145:8 ESV). Our praises recite the great biblical truths about the nature, character, works, purposes, and promises of God. On the basis of this profession of faith, God's people are invited to rejoice in God, to delight in his work, and to trust in his promises. Our thanks gives expression to our gratitude and appreciation for the blessings and benefits that come from his hand. We speak and sing out what God has done particularly for us who assemble together as a community, and what God has done for each of us personally. Thanksgiving to God for the full range of divine gifts and mercies is the natural overflow of a grateful heart.

Consider an exemplary song of praise and thanks from Scripture. Psalm 100:1–5 reads:

> Shout for joy to the LORD, all the earth.
> Worship the LORD with gladness;
>   come before him with joyful songs.
> Know that the LORD is God.
>   It is he who made us, and we are his;
>   we are his people, the sheep of his pasture.
> Enter his gates with thanksgiving
>   and his courts with praise;
>   give thanks to him and praise his name.
> For the LORD is good and his love endures
>   forever; his faithfulness continues
>   through all generations.

This psalm has many features that are central to the practice of praise and thanksgiving. It is brimming with confidence in God. It recognizes the objective fact of the universe, namely, that God is God, and we are not. It refers to his goodness, love, and faithfulness. These qualities of God's moral character have been made manifest in his works of creation and salvation. The psalm makes clear our identity as his people ("sheep") who belong to him and are thoroughly under his care. Its main emotion is confident joy. Many of the Psalms capture the same spiritual dynamics in a rich biblical vocabulary of praise and thanksgiving.

In our worship time together, there should be a spiritual priority of praise. In thinking so I have been influenced by the example of Dr. John Gladstone, a long-time Baptist pastor in Toronto. He had a remarkable custom. John began all his prayers—praying for individuals in their hospital bed, starting a board meeting, leading corporate worship, saying grace at a meal—in the same way. Whatever he was asked to pray for, or pray about, he always started like this:

> Great and marvelous are your deeds,
>   Lord God Almighty.
> Just and true are your ways,
>   King of the nations.
> Who will not fear you, Lord,
>   and bring glory to your name?
> For you alone are holy.
> All nations will come
>   and worship before you,
>   for your righteous acts have been revealed.

Those are the words of Revelation 15:3–4. That was his standard preamble to any and all of his prayers. It is the language of praise, pure and simple. It is declaration of who God is and what he has done. It is a triumphant declaration of God's victory, and assertion of God's incomparable character. This text provides the reframing of any and all subsequent petitions and intercessions that may be offered next. This preamble is the reminder that we need always to keep at the forefront of our thoughts the identity of the One to whom we pray, whenever we pray, lest we distort our faith by remaking God in our own image, by whittling God down to the size that we can comprehend, or to a domesticated, tamed god that we can control or manipulate for our ends.

In addition to the Bible's own testimony of praise about God, there is a wealth of classical hymnody and contemporary songs that are resolutely God-centred in recounting God's greatness, supremacy, holiness, beauty, and love. Think of just a few opening lines from well-known hymns that evoke from us our heart's praise:

- "Rejoice, the Lord is King!"
- "Praise to the Lord, the Almighty, the King of Creation!"
- "To God be the glory, great things he has done!"
- "Great is Thy faithfulness, O God my Father!"

- "Joyful, joyful, we adore Thee, God of glory, Lord of love."
- "Amazing grace, how sweet the sound, that saved a wretch like me!"

Leanne van Dyk reminds us that "hymn texts are su-per-concentrated theology, treasures of compact theological statement. The church that sings excellent hymn texts . . . is being formed in a fine school of faith."[1] Along these lines, worship scholar John Witvliet has suggested that a congregation's singing of what we simply call "the Doxology" carries great implications for forming our faith. He comments, "When we sing 'Praise God from whom all blessings flow,' we are also saying 'Down with the gods from whom no blessings flow.'"[2] He expounds the song as follows:

> Praise God, from whom all blessings flow (and not like any lifeless idol, like the stock market or shopping mall!).
> Praise Him, all creatures here below (because this God is far better than anything we could create from our own imaginations!).

---

1. Leanne van Dyk, introduction to *A More Profound Alleluia: Theology and Worship in Harmony*, ed. Leanne van Dyk (Grand Rapids: Eerdmans, 2005), xvi.

2. John D. Witvliet, "The Opening of Worship: Trinity," in Van Dyk, *A More Profound Alleluia*, 12.

> Praise Him above, ye heavenly host (because even in heaven there is only One worthy of praise!).
>
> Praise Father, Son, and Holy Ghost (because it is the triune God that both promises and effects life-giving redemption). Amen.[3]

The expression of praise and thanks is central to the Christian spiritual-moral life. We remind ourselves whenever we sing hymns like these that the universe does not revolve around us. We are creatures, not the Creator. We live in God's world. God is wonderfully glorious, and we see ourselves rightly only when we see who God is. This praise brings joy, since praise and adoration of God is, after all, what we were made for. It is the expression of our human flourishing. It is our unique vocation of all of God's creatures to give him our praise, in recognition of who he is, out of sheer, overflowing, abundant gratitude.

Many readers will be familiar with St. Augustine's famous statement in his classic autobiography, from the opening sentences of his *Confessions*: "Our hearts are restless until they rest in thee." This speaks to the fulfillment of human nature through relationship with God. That statement seen in the wider context of what Augustine was saying is deeply instructive for our purposes. The full quote goes like this:

3. Ibid., 13.

"You are great, Lord, and highly to be praised" (Ps. 47:2): great is your power and your wisdom is immeasurable (Ps. 146:5). Man, a little piece of your creation, desires to praise you, a human being "bearing his mortality within him" (2 Cor. 4:10), carrying with him the witness of his sin and the witness that you "resist the proud" (1 Pet. 5:5). Nevertheless, to praise you is the desire of man, a little piece of your creation. You stir man to take pleasure in praising you, because you have made us for yourself, and our heart is restless until it rests in you.[4]

Our restless hearts are yearning to praise because we are made for it. The marks of sin and death are, truly, all around us. Think only for a moment about our most recent experience of horrendous tragedies of genocide, terrorism, or natural disasters. Every day's newspapers bring us fresh encounters with suffering, agony, and despair of a sin-torn world. In moral terms, our world has not improved much since Augustine's time.

And yet, God's people lift their heads above the mire. The world was stunned by images a few years back of Christians gathering for worship—indeed, to offer praise!—in burned out, bombed out churches in Egypt. A mere shell of charred structure remained, but God's people gathered there nevertheless, because they were "stirred so deeply"

4. Saint Augustine, *Confessions*, trans. Peter Chadwick (Oxford: Oxford University Press, 1991), 3.

inside themselves, as Augustine puts it, that they cannot do anything else but live out the priority of praise by gathering, despite it all. They continued to sing his praises, no matter what. These Egyptian believers are contemporary practitioners of biblical faith. Recall the case of the apostle Paul and his companion Silas in prison: stripped, beaten with rods, locked in the inner cell, bound with their feet in stocks, and doing what exactly? "Praying and singing hymns to God" (Acts 16:25).

The practice of the priority of praise is not undertaken by sticking one's head in the sand. Making God's praise the starting point for all else is not a way of ignoring the harsh realities of the world, or pretending that the harsh realities of our lives, and our brokenness, are not real. It is the best way to practice faithfulness to the faithful God. It is the best way to maintain a right and true perspective on the suffering of the world. Suffering does not have the last word, after all. God does.

Theologian Karl Barth suggests that gratitude is our most fundamental response to God's grace as human creatures. He says, "We have our being in gratitude."[5] What he means is that giving thanks to God is what is at the very essence of our identity as creatures of God who

5. Karl Barth, *Church Dogmatics*, III/IV, 44, quoted in Peter J. Leithart, "Being in Gratitude," *First Things*, November 25, 2015, https://www.firstthings.com/blogs/leithart/2015/11/being-in-gratitude.

34

have received his blessings. Being grateful is not simply something we do; it is who and what we are. Gratitude becomes our basic way of being in the world, a persistent quality of our ways of thinking, feeling, and responding to our experience. In a real sense, in light of God's amazing grace, human gratitude defines who we are as subjects, as acting creatures in God's world. A historian of gratitude, Peter Leithart, comments that gratitude is so fundamental to human life that we should reject Enlightenment philosopher Rene Descartes's definition of human identity as thinking beings ("I think, therefore I am"), replacing it with a new slogan: "I thank, therefore I am."[6]

This account of praise and thanksgiving is loaded with moral implications. The ongoing practice of praise and thanksgiving is utterly central to the spiritual-moral formation of God's people. Christian character is shaped profoundly by the experience of praise and thanksgiving. Communal worship that praises God no matter what, simply on account of his character and grace, is actually what aligns our hearts and minds with the truest reality of the universe. God is God and therefore is worthy of adoration. How do we learn to be people whose lives are oriented toward God and anchored in him? First and foremost in worship that recites and sings God's praise.

6. Peter Leithart, "Being in Gratitude." See also his *Gratitude: An Intellectual History* (Waco: Baylor University Press, 2014).

The continual practice of thanksgiving for blessings, large or small, is the formation into habits of the heart that constitute our truest human identity. We are creatures who have received blessings at God's hands. Our response is gratitude. As any parent knows, giving thanks is not natural to us. As fallen, sinful creatures, even adorable and tolerably well-behaved children need to be trained to give thanks. How many times does a parent need to remind a child to "say thank you" for something they have been given? Eventually, the hope is that the practice of giving thanks becomes natural to the child, part of their moral character. This goes beyond mere etiquette. It is a matter of a fundamental posture toward life. Gratitude is the Christian alternative to secular culture's deep sense of entitlement. Christians should stand out in their cultural contexts on account of their strange habit of being grateful people, living with a certain joy and freedom that comes from knowing that gift and gratitude are the real dynamics of human life.

6

Repentance and Confession of Sin

Virtually every form of worship throughout history in the Christian tradition has included some expression of confession of sin. God's people sing God's praise, marvel again in his love, mercy, and grace, and thus can only respond, "Woe unto us! Have mercy on us! Help us!" A sense of our unworthiness follows from ascribing worth to God, which is the derivation of the word "worship." Repentance and confession of sin therefore is the appropriate next step in the gospel cycle that forms the heart of orthodox worship. Repentance is sorrow for one's sin and resolve to turn away from it. Confession is stating one's sins and seeking God's forgiveness and cleansing.

Before going any further, it is essential to stress where repentance and confession are situated in the fourfold cycle. Theologian James Torrance makes a critical point when he clarifies that our repentance is a response to grace, not a condition of grace. He cites John Calvin's distinction between "legal repentance" and "evangelical repentance." According to Torrance, legal repentance operates by the slogan, "Repent, and if you repent you will be forgiven" on the assumption that God "has to be conditioned into being gracious. It makes our imperatives of obedience prior to the indicatives of grace, and regards God's love and forgiveness and acceptance as conditional upon what we do." On the other hand, "evangelical repentance" has the slogan, "Christ has borne your sins on the cross, therefore, repent!" This approach understands that repentance is "our response to grace, not a condition of grace. The goodness of God leads us to repentance."[7] This is why our declaration of God's praise logically precedes our repentance and confession of sin.

There are several communal options for confession of sin. Some churches have used silent prayer, a practice that emphasizes the individual's responsibility before God. Others use a set form of words for reciting a corporate confession, an approach that emphasizes the church's solidarity, as no one is exempted from seeing him or herself as in need of repentance. Another option is reading a Scripture text that speaks clearly of repentance, for instance as expressed most clearly in 1 John 1:8–9, "If we claim to be without sin, we deceive ourselves and the truth is not in

7. James B. Torrance, *Worship, Community and the Triune God of Grace* (Downers Grove, IL: InterVarsity, 1996), 54.

us. If we confess our sins, he is faithful and just and will forgive us our sins and purify us from all unrighteousness."

Scripture's teaching reveals the human situation as standing before the righteous and holy God as people whose lives are marked by sin, rebellion, and brokenness. From Genesis 3 onward, the biblical narrative depicts human beings as needing God's forgiveness. Yet the word "sin" is no longer popular and is often trivialized. Many churches studiously avoid it. The idea of "being a sinner" seems not only old-fashioned but also highly unacceptable to contemporary ears. Some people (even churchgoing people) reject this traditional language as offensive. It is sometimes said to be harmful to healthy self-esteem, unduly negative about human potential, or simplistic about the complexities of life.

These modern qualms actually seem naive and dubious when put over against the enduring wisdom expressed by the church's historic theological stance. Since "all have sinned and fall short of the glory of God" (Rom. 3:23), there is serious spiritual risk in dropping the notion of sin or even substituting any other language for "sin." Conformity to the preferences and tolerances of a secularized and post-Christian culture can only lead to a compromised faith.

In moral terms, 1 John points to the heart of matters: self-deception. We are prone to justifying our actions, rationalizing our misconduct, and making excuses for our selfishness and unjust treatment of others. We are inclined toward distorted self-perception. We defy accountability for our actions. We fudge reality in our own favour. Over against this deep-seated pattern of moral obfuscation, the biblical tradition captured by repentance and confession in communal worship is resolutely clear-eyed and blunt about human sinfulness. It is not just that human beings are somewhat flawed or sometimes make mistakes, perhaps occasionally falling short of God's standards. No, we are sinners, which means that our natures are corrupt and in need of radical transformation. The controversial doctrine of "total depravity" does not mean that everything we do is as bad as it could possibly be. Rather, it means that every aspect of our lives is marked in some manner by sinful corruption. The full scope of human activity is twisted by sin and needs redemption. Our defiance of God and his ways requires dramatic intervention, which is the rationale for God's saving action in the cross and resurrection of Jesus. This is why the confession of sin is typically followed immediately in the order of service by a declaration of pardon, an announcement of the gospel message of forgiveness for all those who repent and believe the good news.

How do we become people who are capable of honesty about ourselves? How do we learn to challenge the human tendency toward self-deception, rationalization, and obfuscation of responsibility? It takes deeply formative practices to shape our hearts, imaginations, and moral sensibilities. Where else would someone learn sorrow over their sins? Where else would some gain the language to name their sins and to express remorse and rejection of them? The morally formative power of congregational worship again comes to the forefront. There is no substitute for this ongoing, gradual schooling in the intellectual and emotional maturity it takes to be aware of our sins, and unflinchingly honest about them. The structure of Sunday worship provides a framework of moral accountability unlike any other cultural practice in our world. We hold ourselves to transcendent standards of moral judgment. We make ourselves answerable to divine expectations for our lives, not just our own ideals.

7

Creed

Christian tradition has given a prominent place in corporate worship to reciting a condensed statement of core beliefs. For our purposes, we will focus on how the Apostles' Creed has served this role (leaving aside for now the Nicene Creed). It has been interpreted as composed of twelve statements correlating with the twelve apostles, each of whom was thought to have contributed an article. That alleged connection has no historical validity, but it makes the point that the Apostles' Creed is attested as a summary of apostolic teaching, and thereby carries the extended authority that flows from the apostolic witnesses themselves. The creed has been used for centuries, encapsulating the church's belief since its inception. Alongside the Ten Commandments and the Lord's Prayer, it has been central to the church's pattern of catechesis, its basic instruction forming people in the faith.

Already we can see the formative power of the practice of reciting the creed simply in its ability to unite contemporary Christians in a deeply rooted, long-standing community of faith. We belong to a people whose life is shaped by convictions about truth. By reciting the creed, we disavow any sense that we are able to make up our beliefs for ourselves or make up truths that will satisfy us. We stand in spiritual and practical solidarity with our spiritual mothers and fathers across the centuries and around the world. Our faith is their faith. Therefore even restless souls yearning for "the new and the next" are not at liberty to change the church's confession of faith. We have received this confession as a gift, and we pass it along to our children. Some have likened reciting the creed to taking an oath of citizenship. It declares our allegiance to a particular people who subscribe freely to a very peculiar set of beliefs. This rootedness in the history of God's people is a powerful counterweight to the subjectivism and individualism that can so easily shape our moral outlook.

Everyone's actions reveal our beliefs about the nature of the universe and our place in it. Worship scholar Don Saliers has commented, "When worship occurs, people are characterized, given their life and their fundamental location and orientation in the world."[1] His reference to

1. Don E. Saliers, "Liturgy and Ethics: Some New Beginnings," in *Liturgy and the Moral Self: Humanity at Full Stretch Before God; Essays*

people being "characterized" in worship resonates with our theme: the shaping of character. For people of Christian character, the creed plays a huge part in describing their location and orientation in the world.

Everyone has a worldview or core set of beliefs about reality, the way the world is. This is clearly part of our everyday experience, if we pause even briefly to reflect on how people actually live their lives. There are reasons underlying why people act as they do, for better or for worse. People who believe that the universe is a godless, meaningless, and random place have a hard time justifying why they believe justice is possible or kindness is a virtue. On this worldview, acts of compassion or generosity are quite literally out of step with the universe as they understand it, contrary to the way things really are. Their worldview fits with a me-centred, pleasure-oriented, stay-out-of-my-way-and-let-me-do-my-thing approach to life. If that worldview actually is true, everyone can and should decide what is morally right and good, according to personal preference, since there is no other basis for drawing such conclusions. If there is no God and no transcendent source of meaning or value, morality is a merely human venture focused on convincing people to, as best they can,

---

in Honor of Don E. Saliers, ed. E. Byron Anderson and Bruce T. Morrill (Collegeville, MN: Liturgical Press, 1998), 17; quoted in David L. Stubbs, "Ending of Worship: Ethics," in van Dyk, *A More Profound Alleluia*, 140.

limit their self-interest and aggression for the sake of others. There are no moral standards that are applicable to all people, apart from their own deliberate choice, despite the fact that everyone sees undeniable moral evil around them—rape, genocide, terrorism.

Corporate worship tells a completely different and utterly counter-cultural story. Our lives as Christians emerge over time from immersion into the story of God. Philosopher Alasdair MacIntyre has argued that we can only answer the question "What am I to do?" if we can answer the prior question, "Of what story or stories do I find myself a part?"[2] This is a profound truth about the moral life. The creed reminds us of the basic tenets of the Christian story. How we act in the world should reflect the truths of the story expressed in the creed we confess. As such, the creed is foundational to Christian ethics. The moral life of Christians is not derived from philosophical speculation or personal whim but from the fundamental shape of our historic Christian confession.

> I believe in God, the Father Almighty,
> Creator of heaven and earth.
>
> I believe in Jesus Christ, God's only Son, our Lord,
> who was conceived by the Holy Spirit,

2. Alasdair MacIntyre, *After Virtue: A Study in Moral Theory* (London: Duckworth, 1981), 201.

born of the Virgin Mary,
suffered under Pontius Pilate,
was crucified, died, and was buried;
he descended to the dead.
On the third day he rose again;
he ascended into heaven,
he is seated at the right hand of the Father,
and he will come to judge the living and the dead.

I believe in the Holy Spirit,
the holy catholic church,
the communion of saints,
the forgiveness of sins,
the resurrection of the body,
and the life everlasting. Amen.

It is beyond the scope of this book to provide a full exposition of the creed.[3] We can only highlight a few features that have particularly important moral implications. First, the creed is structured into three paragraphs, each starting "I believe." Our English word "creed" derives from the Latin, *credo*, which simply means "I believe." It refers to our affirmation of a deeply personal trust, not merely our factual belief in God's existence. It is "believ-

3. Succinct treatments include J. I. Packer, *Affirming the Apostles' Creed* (Wheaton, IL: Crossway, 2008); C. E. B. Cranfield, *The Apostles' Creed: A Faith to Live By* (Grand Rapids: Eerdmans, 1993); Justo L. González, *The Apostles' Creed for Today* (Louisville, KY: Westminster John Knox Press, 2007).

ing *in*" rather than merely "believing *that*." Trust implies living a life based on the One who is trusted. When a congregation stands to say the creed together during Sunday worship, we say it individually as a matter of personal conviction ("I believe") yet collectively as an expression of a shared reality. This faith is personal to me, yet not private. It is ours as a congregation, but also mine as a congregant, just as we each confess our individual and personal sins—"I have sinned"—as part of a community that shares that experience so that we together can say, "We have sinned." This practice can only be formative of our personal identity as people who personally trust in God, as part of a community of people who trust in God. We renew that trust on a weekly basis, reinforcing that trust as a core commitment of our hearts, minds, and affections.

Who is trusted? That makes all the difference. The creed points toward the nature and character of the Triune God—Father, Son, and Holy Spirit—as the object of our faith. This schools us in the habits of thinking of God as one God in three persons. The one God is both Creator and Redeemer. By affirming God as Creator, we say that we are living in God's world, which is creation, not merely in "nature." We are creatures, who therefore take our place in a universe that has a transcendent source and whose meaning is found in relationship to its Author. The Creator's design of the universe is the context for our lives in all their fullness, including our social and moral lives. It is inherently humbling to innate human pride to embrace a status as creatures. Our creedal confession speaks of a fundamental dependence upon God, who himself is the source and arbiter of all life, including our life. This takes us back to the core moral issue of trust. In the garden of Eden, our ancestors diverted from the path of active, personal, daily trusting dependence upon God as the good and generous Creator in favour of an ill-fated, self-reliant quest to become "like God" (Gen. 3:5).

The creed also helps us to understand the kind of world the creation really is. In other words, it enables us to imagine where we are. It does so by naming our present and also naming our future as our moral landscape.

The world in which we live is the same place to which Jesus came two millennia ago. It is where he lived, died, and rose from the dead. According to the creed, the climax of the Christian story is the particular history of Jesus of Nazareth, "born of the Virgin Mary." As countless commentators have observed, we are not told any of the details of Jesus's earthly life—only that he was "crucified under Pontius Pilate." Yet the significance of the cross for our spiritual-moral lives can hardly be overstated. The true God, who is at the same time the exemplary human being, was killed by God's own creatures. God's love and goodness appeared in human flesh, but was despised and rejected. How can we not understand that our world unavoidably is a veil of tears? As theologian Herbert Mc-

Cabe has suggested, the fate of Jesus tells us that "the kind of world we have" is a "crucifying world, a world doomed to reject its own meaning."[4]

Yet this same Jesus is risen from the dead, ascended into heaven, and "is coming to judge the living and the dead." This describes to us the future, as does the later phrase confessing that we believe in the "resurrection of the body." Our broken world is still God's world, subject to spiritual-moral accountability to its Creator and Redeemer. Jesus is God's appointed judge. Jesus will exercise divine judgment, reckoning justly and mercifully with the sins of the world. If so, the moral action of every human being must matter. God's world has a future, continuous with this world, in which we are morally answerable for our ways. In his providence and according to his own perfect timing, God will bring his purposes for our world to its ultimate fulfillment in a radically transformed new heavens and new earth (Isa. 65:17; Rev. 21:1).

This narrative tells us where we are and when we are living. We are in God's world: created, redeemed, being redeemed, and awaiting full redemption. We are living between the times, between the time of Jesus's coming and Jesus's return in judgement. This is the context for every aspect of our daily lives. Our moral lives are found in this

4. Herbert McCabe, *Law, Love and Language* (London: Sheed & Ward, 1968), 132.

landscape and in this time zone. (We will return to this insight when we discuss the Lord's Supper.)

In all these ways, and more, the practice of saying the creed turns our attention away from ourselves and toward God. Theologian Karl Barth comments that in reciting the creed, "I see myself completely filled and determined by this object of my faith. And what interests me is not my faith, but He in whom I believe."[5] In our self-preoccupied culture, Christian faith can be distorted by the assumption that what is most important is the subjective strength of my faith or my conquest of any possible doubt. Me-centredness can even creep into the church and its preaching. Christianity can be reduced into a means of getting "your best life now"—with an emphasis on *your*. Reciting the creed is one way of resisting such compromise.

Our creedal confession is that this God, the one who is Creator, who is known in the crucified and risen Jesus, whose Spirit is at work in the church, is the one upon whom we depend. This God is the centre of our lives. We trust him. We pray to live as people who belong to this story—what the Triune God is doing in his world. We conform our hearts, minds, and affections to the truth of this God. This is our aspiration and desire. It sets our spiritual-moral lives on a peculiar path. Therefore it makes

5. Karl Barth, *Dogmatics in Outline* (New York: Harper Torchbooks, 1959), 16.

sense that the creed is actually a prayer concluding with "Amen." We tend to think of the creed too much as a series of abstract theological propositions. No, it is a prayer, summing up our aspirations for trusting in the One True God whose story is the work of God the Father, God the Son, and God the Holy Spirit.

8

Scripture Reading and Sermon

The earliest Christians gathered together to hear the Scriptures of the Hebrew Bible read aloud. The apostle Paul writes to his young protégé Timothy: "Until I come, devote yourself to the public reading of Scripture, to preaching and to teaching" (1 Tim. 4:13). This Christian practice was a continuation of the Jewish pattern of synagogue worship, which involved readings from the law and the prophets (a scene depicted in Acts 13:15). Over the course of Christian history, public worship has standardly included readings from the whole Bible, both Old and New Testaments. Most traditions include at least one reading (often the text for the day's sermon). Those traditions that use a lectionary (that is, a set list of Scripture readings to be used throughout the year) typically include an Old Testament reading, a Psalm, and a New Testament reading. In some traditions, there is both a Gospel reading and an epistle.

The importance of Christians listening attentively to the Scriptures can hardly be overstated. Scripture is "God's Word written."[1] Hearing these Scriptures read is the chief way in which we locate ourselves in God's story. "By having Scripture read in worship, God's people discover that their imaginations are fired, their hopes enlivened, their vision expanded, their sensibilities reformed and refashioned."[2]

The immense value of public readings of Scripture implies that they should be taken seriously and performed well. The segment of a service dedicated to the readings unfortunately can be a time when some congregants tune out by reading the bulletin, making their lunch plans, or checking their phones rather than truly paying full attention to what is being said. Taking the readings seriously means, among other things, that congregations should refuse to let their readers mumble, stumble, and fumble their way through the passage. Neither a droning monotone nor melodramatic flourish is edifying to the hearers. If we agree that listening to God's Word is important, I would suggest that congregations be trained on how to listen to Scripture just as lectors are trained in how to read

1. This phrase is used in the Thirty-Nine Articles of the Anglican Church, paragraph 20.

2. Jim Fodor, "Reading the Scriptures: Rehearsing Identity, Practicing Character," in *The Blackwell Companion to Christian Ethics*, ed. Stanley Hauerwas and Samuel Wells (Oxford: Blackwell, 2006), 141.

it aloud. In a world dominated increasingly by screens, where else do people learn the practical skill of listening well to someone speaking?

We do well to bear in mind that the purpose of Scripture is described by Scripture itself in terms that clearly emphasize moral formation. The most famous text on this topic is 2 Timothy 3:16–17 (ESV), which reads: "All Scripture is breathed out by God and profitable for teaching, for reproof, for correction, and for training in righteousness, that the man of God may be complete, equipped for every good work."

A great deal could be said here about the nature of biblical inspiration and biblical authority. This is a crucial passage for developing a detailed theology of Scripture. Instead my focus more narrowly is on the purpose of the Bible. We can note immediately that the divine purpose of Scripture goes far beyond the simple dissemination of information. Yes, it is the vehicle of divine revelation, but not merely for the sake of passing along propositions to be known in some disinterested or abstract way. The practical usefulness of Scripture is accented in this verse. Scripture's function is to teach us God's truth and God's ways, rebuke our sins, correct our errors and point us in the right direction, and train us for living upright lives. The result of Scripture's work is a transformed life. The outcome of its rejuvenating work is described in thoroughly moral terms: the Christian becomes "mature" and "equipped for every good work." The Greek word *artios* rendered "mature" refers to someone who is whole or complete, someone who has fully grown into his or her divinely intended purpose as a human being. This suggests that the whole person has been shaped through engagement with the Bible—mind, heart, imagination, attitudes, and affections. Such a person has been made ready and is well prepared for every form of work and service as God's representative in God's world. As Eugene Peterson translates 2 Tim. 3:17 in *The Message*: "Through the Word we are put together and shaped up for the tasks God has for us." If so, then failing to attend seriously to the Bible will result in a lack of spiritual-moral maturity. Without the Word we can only be dis-integrated and unshaped for what God has for us.

A great deal is at stake. This understanding of the formative moral purpose of Scripture reminds us of the paramount importance of preaching that expounds God's Word with careful attention to the message of the texts. The biblical story is, first and foremost, the story of who God is and what he has done. It reveals his character to us, and it calls his people, over and over again, to a response of faith, trust, and obedience. The preacher's challenge is to open the Word's meaning to the congregation, allowing the Bible to speak for itself in ways that connect with the context of the listeners. The great Protestant Reformer Martin Luther said, "If you preach the gospel in all aspects with the exception of the issues which deal specifically with your time, you are not preaching the gospel at all."[3] This does not mean distorting the Bible's message for the sake of relevance to social, political, or moral issues. It does not mean reading Marxism or capitalism or anarchism back into the Bible. Rather, it means not missing the contemporary relevance of the Bible's timeless message. The best way to offer morally formative preaching is to allow the Spirit to work through the sermon by exposing and clarifying the Bible's own internal moral logic. The Bible's moral teaching is woven throughout the whole rather than segmented into isolated blocks. Do we have eyes to see it?

Careful attention to the persistent pattern of biblical teaching will reveal that three critical elements are constantly interconnected. On a recurring basis in both Old and New Testaments, biblical texts bring closely together statements related to *believing* (teaching about the nature and character of God and his work), *belonging* to God's community (teaching about God's people and their life together), and *behaving* in distinctive ways that live out the truths of our faith (teaching about ethics and practical action in everyday life). There are countless examples. A pivotal and programmatic text illustrates the pattern.

3. Quoted in Rick Warren, "Build a Bridge between God's Word and Issues of Our Day," Pastors.com, February 26, 2013, http://pastors.com/build-a-bridge-between-gods-word-and-issues-of-our-day/. Accessed September 2, 2016.

When the Israelites arrive at Mount Sinai, the Lord speaks to Moses.

> The LORD called to him out of the mountain, saying, "Thus you shall say to the house of Jacob, and tell the people of Israel: 'You yourselves have seen what I did to the Egyptians, and how I bore you on eagles' wings and brought you to myself. Now therefore, if you will indeed obey my voice and keep my covenant, you shall be my treasured possession among all peoples, for all the earth is mine; and you shall be to me a kingdom of priests and a holy nation.' These are the words that you shall speak to the people of Israel." (Exod. 19:3–6 ESV)

This passage holds tightly together our three integrated, mutually dependent realities. In the realm of belief, the Lord's own character and action is described—what he has done in the exodus from Egypt. The Israelites are called to *belief* and trust in this God, who says he has "brought you to myself." Yahweh's mighty act of deliverance is the basis for his relationship with Israel, which in the realm of *belonging* makes Israel "a kingdom of priests and a holy nation." Inherent to Israel's response to their salvation through God's power is their *behaviour* in obedience. Yahweh calls them to "obey my voice and keep my covenant." Putting together the key idea of the passage in terms of these three facets of text, we can say that the point is this: trusting belief in who God is and what he has done in salvation constitutes a new community that is called to obedience and holiness.

This passage is a prime example of what I mean by speaking of the Bible's own internal moral logic, which is found throughout the Old and New Testaments. Embedded in virtually every biblical passage are these three integrated components. They do not appear always in the same way. There is not necessarily a predictable sequence to express the logic. Sometimes one aspect or another gets considerably more emphasis. Sometimes as readers or preachers we fail to see the text's own connections to the practical and ethical implications. But they are virtually always there to be seen, if we are attentive readers. We will find that the moral teaching of the Bible is always grounded in God's character and faithful action, and is always expressed as the vocation of God's faithful people. In conceptual terms, Christian ethics is always rooted in theology (teaching about God) and in ecclesiology (teaching about the church). From this standpoint, our exploration of the ways in which corporate worship shapes Christian character is simply a meditation on one aspect of ecclesiology.

Knowing the internal moral logic of the Bible, and that the Scriptures are intended by God to foster our maturity and readiness for good works, should prevent preachers from the temptation to impose any kind of alien moral agenda upon the Bible. At the same time, this realization should prevent them from neglecting the moral message that is so commonly centrally embedded in the flow of thought. Attention to Scripture is essential for the formation of God's people for God's work.

9

Lord's Prayer and Intercessions

The importance of the Lord's Prayer in the Christian tradition can hardly be overstated. It is the paradigm of all Christian prayer. It is the only prayer that Jesus taught his disciples to pray. Whether it is used as a set form of words or as a pattern for other prayers, the core meaning and structure of the Lord's Prayer should provide the framework for every congregation's prayers each week.

Christian moral formation is about how the whole person takes on Christ-like character. The great intermediary between our beliefs and our behaviour is the essential spring of our actions, namely, our desires. All our words and actions flow from the core of being, what Scripture calls our heart. Jesus teaches, "A good man brings good things out of the good stored up in his heart, and an evil man brings evil things out of the evil stored up in his heart. For the mouth speaks what the heart is full of" (Luke 6:45).

What transforms our hearts? Surely the work of God's Spirit. What means does God's Spirit use to soften, mould, and renovate our hearts? Prayer, first and foremost. Prayer aligns our desires with God's heart. Through the Lord's Prayer, Jesus rearranges our desires by bringing them into harmony with his desires. If our character is to become like Christ, and our actions are to reflect the way of life modeled by Christ, then our desires need to become more and more like Christ's desires. Nothing does that as thoroughly as praying the Lord's Prayer.

Elsewhere I have given extended discussion to the Lord's Prayer.[1] This chapter will highlight the formative dimension of using this prayer in corporate worship. It begins by naming our identity: we belong to our heavenly Father. We are not alone. We are not orphans in the world. We have a Father who loves us. We can talk with him. His heart is open to us. What we pray for is our loving, listening heavenly Father's priorities for his people.

It is widely recognized that the prayer has two halves. My interpretation of the prayer suggests that there is an ends-means structure. The first half of the prayer resets our priorities toward honouring God's name, kingdom, and will. This names what we are meant to live for. It is like a pledge of allegiance or an oath of citizenship. We express our loyalty to God's purposes in and through Jesus. We learn to put God first through praying these

1. Jeffrey P. Greenman, *The Lord's Prayer* (Cambridge, England: Grove Books, 2012).

words, week by week, year by year. Gradually the work of the Spirit moulds us into people who live first for God and God's agenda. We learn to rethink our own agenda in light of God's priorities and purposes.

The second half of the prayer asks God to give us what his necessary to live for those purposes. We ask God for provision, pardon, and protection so that we can truly live as kingdom-oriented people. It assumes that we cannot possibly make God's name, kingdom, and will our highest priority in life in our own strength. We need God's help to do so. The petitions for daily bread, forgiveness of sins, avoidance of temptation, and deliverance from evil combine to encompass the full range of our earthly experience. These topics in prayer involve every aspect of our lives—physical, relational, moral, spiritual, communal. In each area, the Lord's Prayer expresses utter dependence on God.

Seeing the Lord's Prayer as the paradigm of all prayer means that our other prayers and intercessions—our pleadings on behalf of the needs of the world—are to be consistent with this basic meaning and structure. It is a greatly formative practice to pray for others, including for strangers. Where else do we learn compassion for the sufferings of people? How else are we trained to care about people's deepest needs? The question then arises: What do we actually pray for these folks, near and far? Our moral formation involves seeing others as through God's eyes of love. This means setting aside our own self-focus, eschewing our self-satisfaction, and reaching beyond our indifference. A congregation's intercessions are a potent force for reshaping our desires, even as they bring others into God's presence. Again, we are praying for *them*, but the by-product of our intercessions is God's formation of *us* in the process.

Do our prayers reflect the desire to align ourselves with God's priorities—his name, his kingdom, his will? Do our prayers seek above all else for God's honour and reputation to be triumphant, everywhere, on earth as in heaven? Do we pray for people to be active agents of the kingdom, dependent upon the Lord fully in every area of life, living out God's priorities?

Sometimes our prayers can become conformed to the spirit of our culture, "squeezed into the world's mould" (as J. B. Phillips translates Romans 12:2). Whenever our prayers gravitate toward comfort and convenience, or toward ease and success, or toward our fame and fortune, we have wandered away from the meaning and structure of the Lord's Prayer. Our hearts can be deformed by misguided prayers; misshapen hearts can only lead to disoriented desires that take away from the path that leads to true life in Jesus. This is another reminder of how much is at stake in the practices of communal worship. Accordingly, it would seem wise to keep very close company with the Lord's Prayer.

10

Offertory

The offertory is a standard component of congregational worship during which tithes or financial offerings are collected and then dedicated in some way to God's service with a prayer. Unfortunately it is the most overlooked and least considered element in the entire order of service. The offertory almost always is something that just happens, and few people give it much thought. Some churches effectively downplay the importance of what is happening by deliberately distracting people through giving the weekly announcements or notices during that time. Often the taking up of people's offerings feels mechanical and disconnected from the rest of the service. Many treat it as a mundane necessity of church budgets and not as an expression of worship. This situation should not surprise us much, however, given that most Western Protestant congregations studiously avoid talking directly about money. Jesus talked constantly about money, but most pastors are quite uncomfortable doing so at all. This gap leaves many Christians quite ill-equipped to treat money in ways that reflect their faith, and paves the way for a less-than-intentional offertory practice.

What is morally formative is the weekly practice of giving away our money because we understand ourselves as people of faith who know and worship a God who is amazingly generous and utterly trustworthy. The deliberate, embodied, and communal expression of trusting God enough to give away our money reconfigures our heart, mind, attitudes, and imagination. If we take the offertory seriously, it is an occasion when we remind ourselves that God faithfully provides for our needs; therefore, we need not clutch our material possessions tightly. We are set free by the generosity of God to be generous ourselves. We model ourselves after God's own example, becoming his imitators. We give because he gave and gives and will give. We can act on the basis of that confidence.

The biblical insight is that what we do with our wallets forms our hearts in deeper ways than we think. Jesus said, "Where your treasure is, there your heart will be also" (Matt. 6:21). Putting pieces of our treasure, even quite modest amounts, into the offering basket week by week orients our hearts toward clinging less tenaciously to our material goods and wealth. Passing the basket from one person to another reminds us all that we are not able to generate the means necessary for our own lives. We are dependent creatures. What we have is not our own, despite all appearances to the contrary. In spiritual-moral terms, we live by God's gifts. We are stewards and trustees of what God has given us, nothing more and nothing less. As such, the giving of tithes and offerings exemplifies in congregational worship the sacrificial self-offering that is at the heart of worship in the deepest, truest, all-of-life sense. By giving away our money, we are, in a tangible way, entrusting ourselves afresh to God's mercy and protection. Thus it is suitable for a worship leader to say something like this: "Lord, all that we have comes from you. We praise you as our Provider. We give you this offering today. With it we worship you and give our whole selves to you."

The weekly practice of offering our money to God's service trains us in the peculiar habits of whole-life discipleship. We learn that what we do with our money is really a matter of worship, an indicator of our allegiance to God. In fact, one of the best barometers of our spiritual health is what we do with our money in all areas of life. And if that is true, then what we do with our money on Sunday has tremendous significance. Our practice of giving away money as an act of worship can and should shape what we do with our money during the rest of the week. This changes the moral landscape in which money is located. How is what we spend on clothes, movies, or groceries an expression of worship?

Obviously this God-centred picture is profoundly at odds with how the world sees money. Western Christians are under immense cultural pressure to put money at the centre of our lives. Money is a powerful idol demanding our worship. Everywhere we turn, sometimes quite explicitly, we are invited repeatedly to love money more than anything else, to measure people based on how much money they have, and to see money as something to which we are entitled in a strong sense. In such a culture, we need to recall what Jesus said: "No one can serve two masters. Either you will hate the one and love the other, or you will be devoted to the one and despise the other. You cannot serve both God and money" (Matt. 6:24). The offertory during Sunday worship helps us to remember our truest identity by embodying the practice of denying the tyrannical rule of mammon and by gladly embracing the godly foolishness of generously giving away our money because God is God, and we are not.

11

Lord's Supper or Holy Communion

The focal point of Christian worship historically has been the Lord's Supper, Eucharist, or Holy Communion. Whatever it is called in your tradition, and whether you consider it a sacrament or a rite or an ordinance, the remembrance of Jesus through bread and wine has been indispensably important to Christian formation.[1] There are many complex theological and ecclesial issues related to how the Lord's Supper is understood and practiced that lie beyond the scope of this book. Our focus is upon how participation in the Lord's Supper shapes Christian char-

1. See Gordon T. Smith, *A Holy Meal: The Lord's Supper in the Life of the Church* (Grand Rapids: Baker Academic, 2005); Gordon T. Smith and Jeffrey Gros, *The Lord's Supper: Five Views* (Downers Grove, IL: IVP Academic, 2008).

acter, which naturally hinges upon some understanding of the core meaning of the Supper itself.

Theologian Daniel Migliore provides a helpful summary when he writes, "For most Protestants, the Lord's Supper is primarily a meal in which the self-gift of God in Christ is remembered, celebrated, and proclaimed until Christ comes in glory."[2] A number of key elements of spiritual-moral formation are embedded in that statement. This chapter will unpack Migliore's statement by focusing on the Supper as a communal meal, explaining the significance of God's self-gift, suggesting what it means to be "remembered, celebrated, and proclaimed," and proposing that the Lord's Supper locates Christian experience in time.

First, it is helpful to understand the Lord's Supper as a communal meal. In some circles, attention to the spiritual nature of the event shrouds the reality that what we are doing is eating and drinking. This is something we undertake as embodied creatures. We partake of bread and wine, setting them aside from common usage through prayer in order to play a very specific role in our religious life. We do this together, as a community. In doing so, we identify with what God's people have done over many centuries. We continue their pattern, since we belong to a

2. Daniel Migliore, *Faith Seeking Understanding: An Introduction to Christian Theology* (Grand Rapids: Eerdmans, 2004), 291–92.

people with an extended history over time. More particularly, we belong with this body, with these people, in this place, here and now. We locate our individual identity by breaking bread and drinking wine with them. In some traditions, this emphasis on shared, communal experience is demonstrated by the practice of holding pieces of bread or small cups of juice until everyone has their own so that everyone can eat together simultaneously. In other churches, the commonality of the meal is symbolized as people eat pieces of bread torn from a common loaf and drink from a common cup. Whatever the mode of distribution, the point is that we are not acting as isolated individuals but participating in a shared practice. The meal is a powerful reminder that we are embodied, historical, and communal beings. The practice of the Lord's Supper thereby forms us toward a quite different identity from people bound to the basically gnostic, ahistorical, and individualistic narratives of secular culture.

Second, Migliore's summary rightly puts "the self-gift of God in Christ" at the centre of Eucharistic practice. Every time the Lord's Supper is undertaken, we bear witness to the reality that God is a generous, gracious, and self-giving God. He gives himself to his world. That is his fundamental moral character. The Father sends the Son as his gift; the Father and the Son send the Holy Spirit as a gift. The supreme gift of God is the life and death of Jesus.

The incarnation, life, and death of Jesus of Nazareth demonstrate the nature of divine generosity in mind-boggling ways. Long-time churchgoers can become immune to the shocking nature of this staggering truth. This is not something anyone would ever make up. It is sheer miracle. For our purposes, we need to recall that the basic narrative of the gospel tells the dramatic story in unmistakably moral terms, so that when we partake of the Lord's Supper, we encounter the moral meaning of the gospel of a self-giving God. Consider Paul's "master story" of the gospel in Philippians 2:5–11 (ESV):

> Have this mind among yourselves, which is yours in Christ Jesus, who, though he was in the form of God, did not count equality with God a thing to be grasped, but emptied himself, by taking the form of a servant, being born in the likeness of men. And being found in human form, he humbled himself by becoming obedient to the point of death, even death on a cross. Therefore God has highly exalted him and bestowed on him the name that is above every name, so that at the name of Jesus every knee should bow, in heaven and on earth and under the earth, and every tongue confess that Jesus Christ is Lord, to the glory of God the Father.

Based on this story, Paul teaches that Christians are to conform their lives to the pattern shown by Jesus. What pattern? Generous, sacrificial, other-focused, self-giving love. Why? Because that is how we reflect Christlikeness in the world. Just two verses before this great hymn to Christ, Paul writes, "Do nothing from selfish ambition or conceit, but in humility count others more significant than yourselves. Let each of you look not only to his own interests, but also to the interests of others" (vv. 3–4 ESV). This is what Christ did. He counted others more significant than himself in his life and death. He looked not to his own interests, but to the interests of others. So should we.

The phrase "did not count equality with God a thing to be grasped" is loaded with theological and moral significance.[3] It shows us that God's own character is not to use his unique position, power, and authority for his own advantage or self-interest. Some interpreters have argued that an accurate rendering of Paul's meaning would be, "he did not exploit his position for his own gain." Instead, he emptied himself. The Greek word here is *kenosis*, a rich term for the self-giving of God in the incarnation of Jesus. Jesus does not lose his divinity through self-renunciation, but instead takes on our humanity, paradoxically and wonderfully being simultaneously fully divine and fully human. Furthermore, the God-made-man Jesus

3. For more exposition, see Michael J. Gorman, *Inhabiting the Cruciform God: Kenosis, Justification, and Theosis in Paul's Narrative Soteriology* (Grand Rapids: Eerdmans, 2009).

further humbles himself, even to the point of death. His self-giving is complete. He holds nothing back in his love for humanity.

This is the story that is embedded in the observance of the Lord's Supper. Each time we receive bread and wine, we recall the unique work of Jesus in offering us God's self-gift on the cross. The Eucharist carries morally formative power as it is the main way that Christians, week by week, encounter the self-giving, others-focused, love of Jesus. We are called to model our lives, through the Spirit's power, upon his example.

This story of God's truly amazing self-gift in the incarnation, life, death, and resurrection of Jesus is "remembered, celebrated, and proclaimed" each time we observe the Lord's Supper. Each of those terms is worth exploring briefly: remembrance, celebration, and proclamation. Each is involved as we retell the story of Christ's self-giving in the words of institution and the prayers we offer as we partake of bread and wine. Each is involved as we re-enact what Jesus himself did on the night he was betrayed, when he initiated this sacred meal.

The gospel story of divine self-giving is *remembered* in a distinctive way at the Lord's Supper. The earliest reference we have to the practice comes from Paul's teaching to the church at Corinth. He writes in 1 Corinthians 11:23–26:

> For I received from the Lord what I also passed on to you: The Lord Jesus, on the night he was betrayed, took bread, and when he had given thanks, he broke it and said, "This is my body, which is for you; do this in remembrance of me." In the same way, after supper he took the cup, saying, "This cup is the new covenant in my blood; do this, whenever you drink it, in remembrance of me." For whenever you eat this bread and drink this cup, you proclaim the Lord's death until he comes.

"Do this in remembrance of me." Jesus instituted this practice in order for his broken body and shed blood to be remembered by his followers. At the very least, this means that what he has done on the cross will never be forgotten by his own people. Actually, Torrance reminds us, the Greek word used here (*anamnesis*) "does not simply denote recollecting some remote date of bygone history, as every schoolchild remembers AD 1066 or 1492. Rather, it means remembering in such a way that we see our participation in the past event and see our destiny and future as bound up with it."[4] Remembrance in this deeper sense is our present-day participation through the Holy Spirit in the saving and sanctifying benefits that flow from Christ's cross, where he takes our sin upon himself so that he might be forgiven. We come to Jesus with our hands

---

4. Torrance, *Worship, Community*, 84–85.

literally open before him. That is a posture of humility and dependence. As we sit or stand or kneel to "receive communion" in bread and wine, we experience communion with Christ in the sense of fellowship and sharing in life. This is remembrance in a deeper sense.

At the same time, the remembrance is a *celebration*, a thanksgiving. That is the core meaning of the term Eucharist. Unfortunately there is a tendency in some churches to allow their well-intended solemnity associated with the Lord's Supper to come across as a joyless, drab, monotonous experience. The occasion is serious, of course. We dare not trivialize it. But if the event feels more like a divine defeat than a divine victory, and if there are no signs of joyous celebration of the gospel, surely something important is missing. The Lord's Supper is a visible demonstration of the gospel's sheer miracle. God gives himself for us—alleluia! We are benefactors in what the Reformer John Calvin called the "wonderful exchange," as Torrance explains, "that Christ took what was ours that he might give us what is his."[5] If that is not cause for heartfelt and exuberant praise and thanks, then our faith has gone cold.

The congregation's rehearsal of the Lord's Supper also is a *proclamation*. What is being proclaimed? "The Lord's death." The cross of Jesus is the heart of the gospel. There is no gospel without the cross. As Paul says to the Corin-

5. Torrance, *Worship, Community*, 89.

thians, "I resolved to know nothing while I was with you except Jesus Christ and him crucified" (1 Cor. 2:2). Simply reading Jesus's words of institution, or some other prayer that recounts his death for our sake, preaches the gospel. It proclaims that Jesus, the Word made flesh, gave himself for the sins of the whole world.

It is not just the prayerful words of institution, typically said by the pastor who is leading the service, that "proclaim the Lord's death." The whole event does so. There is a long tradition going back to St. Augustine that understands the Eucharistic feast as "visible words." The actions we perform—breaking bread, eating it, pouring wine, drinking it—are dramatic ways of acting out the words of the Scriptures. The whole complex of words and deeds is what we might call an "object lesson" for the congregation. It is more than an illustration. The message and meaning of Jesus's death is built around the physical objects we see on the table. In this case, the bread and wine are representations of Jesus's own body and blood. And we do not merely see them. We handle them. We experience the objects intimately when we eat and drink them. This experience goes far beyond mere mental recollection. We hear, see, touch, smell, and taste. The whole person is engaged. No wonder the Lord's Supper carries such deep formative power for God's people. This is the spiritual food that nourishes our souls for faithfulness to Christ. In the words of John Calvin: "As bread nourishes, sustains, and protects our bodily life, so the body of Christ is the only food to invigorate and keep alive the soul."[6]

Finally, I want to suggest that the Lord's Supper re-orients the Christian's sense of time. I have claimed that the question "Where are we?" is critical to moral reflection. We live in God's creation. The world is no accident. All people are accountable to our Creator. I have also said that the question, "What story are we part of?" has central significance for morality. We live out the stories that shape our identity. We find ourselves in the story of God's work in creation, redemption, and new creation. The story of Jesus is the centrepiece of the Grand Story of God. Embedded in the Grand Story is a recalculation of time. "What time is it?" also carries a great deal of moral weight. The Eucharist positions the Christian in time—in fact, in between times.

The celebration of the Lord's Supper involves intentionally looking backward toward the past. "Do this in remembrance of me" points to Jesus's work on the cross outside Jerusalem some two thousand years ago. These are very familiar words. We recount ancient history. Yet we participate in the benefits of that long ago event by the Spirit's work today. And at the same time, virtually in the same breath, we "proclaim the Lord's death until he comes." This turns our attention forward in time. We

6. John Calvin, *Institutes of the Christian Religion*, 4.17.3.

anticipate the promised return of Christ to bring God's purposes to their fullness in the new heavens and new earth. That proclamation forces us to look ahead, toward the future time when we will share in the "wedding supper of the Lamb" (Rev. 19:9), the great eschatological banquet. The present time in which we seek to live as faithful followers of Jesus is "the time between the times." We live now on account of the past, experiencing the current blessings of what Christ did. The past is present to us. And so is the future. We live now indwelt by the Holy Spirit, participating already in the blessings of the age to come, even if imperfectly. Nothing captures so simply yet so memorably what we might call "theological time" as the Lord's Supper. Our present life participates in the past and in the future. We know *when* we are, as well as *where* we are.

There is an inexhaustible richness to the Lord's Supper. This short chapter can only begin to sketch some of its importance for our Christian lives. It is like a many faceted jewel that reveals more of its nature when we look at it from many angles. Biblical scholar Markus Barth sparks our imaginations when he writes:

> It is difficult to describe with one term the relationship between the festival act of celebrating the Lord's Supper and the daily activities and sufferings of Christians. Is the Supper a school, an exercise, a training ground, an example to be imitated, a

demonstration and display, the criterion and test, the summit of a mountain or a pyramid, the source that supplies strength and anticipation of the heavenly joys as final reward? Each of these descriptions may contain a grain of truth.[7]

7. Markus Barth, *Rediscovering the Lord's Supper: Communion with Israel, with Christ, and among the Guests* (Eugene, OR: Wipf & Stock, 2006), 76.

Blessing and Dismissal

Does your Sunday worship service simply come to an end, or does it come to a meaningful conclusion? What is said and done at the finish of the appointed order for the day? If the pastor or worship leader says, "Great, that's it, folks. I'm glad everyone had a good time. Let's have some coffee!" that sends a clear message about what the experience was all about. The categories of entertainment and consumption are prominent.

Ideally there should be a well-crafted theological rationale for the entire sequence of elements in a service. There are reasons why traditional orthodox patterns of worship have included elements of blessing and dismissal at the conclusion of an order of service. It makes spiritual sense for words of blessing to precede words of dismissal.

The value of a blessing—words spoken to pronounce God's grace and provision—is that it reminds us that we do not live our lives out of our own puny, frail human resources. We cannot live lives that are pleasing to God by human willpower and sheer determination to be good people. Therefore it is highly important that before we leave the building to resume our everyday lives with all their diverse challenges, we pause to hear again who God is and who we are. What is said should put clearly into our hearts and minds that we actually live under the rich and abundant blessing of the Blessed God, who is Father, Son, and Holy Spirit. Trinitarian invocations provide a powerful way to start and conclude congregational worship. God has given us everything we need. He has given us himself in Jesus Christ. He has spoken to us his Word and fed us at his table. We are equipped by the gracious, generous, gifting God to live out an active faith and trust in him. This divine provision constitutes the foundation and resources for the Christian moral life.

There are many biblical texts that could be used to convey some manner of divine blessing. I will mention just two particularly common passages. The apostle Paul writes in 2 Cor. 13:14, "May the grace of the Lord Jesus Christ, and the love of God, and the fellowship of the Holy Spirit be with you all." The familiar simplicity of this blessing makes it appealing. These are very powerful words linking the Triune God to our concrete, earthly existence.

Another text that is often used in blessings is a truly remarkable one in Numbers 6:22–26. These are powerful words especially since they are Yahweh's own words through Moses whereby God himself blesses his people.

> The Lord said to Moses, "Tell Aaron and his
> sons, 'This is how you are to bless the
> Israelites. Say to them:
> "The Lord bless you
> and keep you;
> the Lord make his face shine on you
> and be gracious to you;
> the Lord turn his face toward you
> and give you peace."'"

This passage brings us the gracious blessing of God himself, which keeps us safe and allows us to live in *shalom*—the condition of well-being, wholeness, and completeness. We cannot generate our own *shalom*. It is a gift.

Knowing that we are blessed by God makes it possible to take up the challenge of being Christ's people in the world. We gather Sunday by Sunday to praise God, hear his Word, be fed at his table, and be equipped for his service. Then what? Where do we go? Not simply into the foyer to drink coffee. We are headed back into the world. We are scattered into every area of society on Monday through Saturday. The complex tasks of being a parent, employee, and citizen face us. Moral complexities face us daily in our worldly duties and ordinary encounters.

The element of dismissal at the end of an order of service is all about this scattering into the world. In theological terms, it is important that congregants do not merely leave the service—they are commissioned. People do not wander away on their own to do whatever they wish but are sent out with a clear purpose. In Christian tradition, the element of dismissal at the end of worship has a rich meaning. The Latin derivation of the word "dismissal" comes from "mission," which refers to our being "sent out" as God's people into God's world to do God's work. This reflects the identity of God's people as representatives of God in the world, his authorized agents. Jesus said to his followers, "As the Father has sent me, I am sending you" (John 20:21). The element of dismissal captures this priority for God's people. To omit this, or to orient our closing words toward fun and coffee, is to miss an opportunity to form our imaginations for God's service.

I know that one church uses the formula, "Our worship has ended; our service begins." This clever slogan is helpful, as far as it reminds the congregation that the horizon ahead of them in the world is the realm of Christian service. Again, a robust Trinitarianism roots our dismissal (action) in the identity of God, which forms our identity (being). Ideally words of blessing would flow into words of commissioning and sending, such as, "Send us out in the power of the Spirit to live and work to your praise and glory." Such a phrase encapsulates the united sense of being sent (with a divine purpose), being empowered by God's Spirit (not living out of our own resources), and living all of life (including our daily work) for the sake of God, for his praise and glory (not for our own fame or glory). This is a radical reorienting in a Godward direction as we take up God's service. It sets the stage for everything we encounter in the scattered life of the church in the world. It reflects our identity as participants in God's own mission to the world, each of us taking up our particular place in it, whatever that might be.

Conclusion

This book provides the basis for concluding that pastors, worship leaders, and lay leaders in congregations (such as elders or deacons) should be more attentive and intentional about the powerful dynamics of congregational worship for whole-life discipleship. If we care about spiritual-moral formation, we need to care about how we worship. Congregational worship is a pedagogy, a school, a training ground, a powerful context for lifelong learning to become God's faithful people. What we sing, pray, read, preach, and do with our bodies in corporate worship Sunday by Sunday has immense significance for shaping people toward Christian faithfulness in all its dimensions.

Here I suggest five guiding questions that could spark useful discussion at a congregational level about our corporate worship. Pastors, worship leaders, and lay leaders (elders and deacons) might take up these questions as they review their congregation's practices of worship.

Conclusion

1. Is our worship resolutely God centred?
    *   Is it clear that our focus is on the honour, glory, and praise of the Triune God?
    *   Is the character and work of each of the three divine persons clearly on display?
    *   Are there any signs of unhelpful me-centredness?
    *   Are there any signs of distortion conforming to the spirit of our age by capitulation to entertainment?
2. How are we telling God's story?
    *   Is there attention to the full biblical account of God's purposes in creation, redemption, and new creation?
    *   Is there sufficient attention to both Old and New Testaments?
3. How is the gospel being re-enacted?
    *   Is it clear that the gospel is truly good news?
    *   Is the gospel portrayed as forming a counter-cultural people?
    *   How is the congregation re-engaging the gospel story each week?
    *   How does our approach to the Lord's Supper re-enact the gospel?
    *   Do our forms of worship "help people to apprehend the worship and ministry of Christ

as he draws us by the Spirit into a life of shared communion, or do they hinder?"[1]

4. What is being modeled for the congregation?
   - What priorities for Christian spirituality are depicted and enacted by the worship service?
   - How is the Bible being treated?
   - How are we hearing and receiving God's word?
   - What kinds of prayers are given most attention? Who is prayed for? Who does the praying?

5. How are lives being shaped by what we do?
   - Does our worship engage the whole person—heart, mind, soul, and strength?
   - How does our worship engage the imagination?
   - What bodily actions are involved? When are people sitting, standing, kneeling, moving, touching each other?
   - Is it clear that the gathering on Sunday for edification leads to active missional engagement in Christian witness and service?

1. Torrance, *Worship, Community*, 15.

For Further Reading

Hauerwas, Stanley, and Samuel Wells, eds. *The Blackwell Companion to Christian Ethics*. Oxford: Blackwell, 2006.

Smith, James K. A. *Desiring the Kingdom: Worship, Worldview, and Culture Formation*. Grand Rapids: Baker Academic, 2009.

———. *Imagining the Kingdom: How Worship Works*. Grand Rapids: Baker Academic, 2013

Torrance, James B. *Worship, Community and the Triune God of Grace*. Downers Grove, IL: InterVarsity, 1996.

Van Dyk, Leanne, ed. *A More Profound Alleluia: Theology and Worship in Harmony*. Grand Rapids: Eerdmans, 2005.

CPSIA information can be obtained at www.ICGtesting.com
Printed in the USA
LVOW07s1046191016

509298LV00001B/1/P